The Book of Truth

"I AM"

Truth iTellit

Contents

Contents

Awareness

Why this book? I could give you many different reasons why this book is beneficial. The most important one: It saves your time.

Nothing on this planet is more valuable than time. This book saves your time and it takes you beyond the mind. It saves your energy and takes you beyond fear. It helps you become aware of the most important thing and being in existence—YOU. It will save you several years and, possibly, even lifetimes of searching. Ultimately, helping you realize YOU ARE exactly what you are searching for. In the words of Eckhart Tolle, "You get there by realizing you are already there."

Your mind strives to find the divine that already exists within you. *The Book of Truth* is a guide to help all of us come to that realization even sooner, while simultaneously pointing us beyond the body and the mind to realize who we truly are.

We live in a time filled with distractions. We live in a generation that has attention deficiency, literally an attention span of little to none. We would rather watch videos and TV shows than read. Therefore, I wrote a book that you wouldn't have to put down because it's boring or long. It avoids jargon and empty words, so you don't have to skip chapters. It's meant to be a short yet powerful text.

If are able to take these written words beyond its pages, your life will transform. And as a result of this transformation, you will be free, at peace, happy and fulfilled. But, in order to do so, it is vital for you to know that these words are not for you to believe. In fact, beliefs do not require realization. Beliefs are information that you accept to be true from one source or another. The purpose of these words is to point you back to your true self. It is not my desire to be "believed" but to help you clearly see who you really are.

I've spent the last seven plus years researching, seeking, praying, traveling, reflecting and meditating. In that time, I studied all of the major religions, philosophies, theologies, mythologies and spiritual practices, both old and new. After seminars, seminary, sleepless nights, fear, pain, confusion, frustration, shame and guilt, I finally have developed the courage to release my words. Words that can only be a confirmation of realization and experience. Words that the human ego can't accept. Words that if you affirm most people will think you are crazy. That's why this book is meant to give you the courage to declare, express and be who you really are. The goal of this book is to point you back home to your true self. There is no introduction to this book because the only introduction for words such as these is **life**. Birth is the introduction of this book and your life is the realization of it. So, once again, why this book? Let's uncover why segment by segment, page by page.

Awakening

In the words of Osho, "Life is contradictory, so truth cannot be uncontradictory; only lies can be uncontradictory, only lies can be consistent. Truth is bound to be inconsistent, because it has to cover everything is in life. It has to be total. And life is contradictory. Don't ask me how I am going to reconcile these two. I am not going to. I am never for reconciliation, and I am not for noncontradictory statements. They are stupid and childish. Life is contradictory and that's why life is alive. Only death is consistent and noncontradictory."

The very nature of who we are is contradictory. The body dies but the spirit—who we really are—lives forever. That is contradictory. Most Christians claim that God is the Father and the Son. That is contradictory.

In this book, I use the term "God" interchangeably. In one context, I may be speaking of the biblical God, the God of religion. The God that came from the human ego. The God that you have been taught about. In another instance, I'll use the term to point to who you really are. I'll use it speaking of your true self, your true nature. Therefore, it is key to be aware of the context I'm writing from and how I use different terms.

Throughout this book, I reference the Bible several times. The Bible is a book of codes and principles hidden in parables, fables. When you take the parables literally you leave the treasure for the chest. The people nor the parables are greater than the principles.

The Bible is nothing but mythology that turned into theology. In other words, it is coded stories and parables. It is to help you understand the universe is working for you, through you and as you. I do not reference these parables as if they are true, or really happened. I reference the scriptures because I have come to the realization that the Bible is the most well-known book of our time. It is also the most misused and misunderstood book of our time. It has been used for evil, prejudices, racism, sexism and many other things. I personally believe all information can be used for evil or for good.

Again, I reference the Bible because of the astrology, philosophy and principles coded in the fables, stories. The stories are meaningless without the substance underneath them. Therefore, I use them only to reveal and help point to who you are. Yes. I know, I know. Using fiction to point to facts is contradictory. Using myths to create awareness is contradictory. So, it is key to realize that the truth can appear contradictory to the ego. Note, that regardless of who or what I'm quoting, I'm only doing so to point you back home to yourself. Hence, I use them not as a proof of truth but as a reference.

This realization didn't come from any religion, Bible or holy book. It didn't come from

Jesus, Buddha, Abraham or any other man. It came from within my own being. As a result, I am fully capable of understanding those books and people.

Finally you have a book that isn't about history, science, biology, economics, government, or religion. You finally have a book that is for **YOU.** In school and even in college we are taught about the world, technology, business, marketing, history and many other meaningless things. Yet, we forget the most important thing of all, ourselves. This book will not leave you out, this book will not put anyone or anything before you. You are the only absolute truth. This book nor any book, words, scripture or creed can be the truth. You are the truth.

Therefore, the purpose of this short book is to help point you to the truth, yourself. Now you may be wondering why I titled this *The Book of Truth* when no words can be the truth. This too is contradictory but so is anything written or spoken about who you really are. The mind tries to define something that words can't describe. In actuality I am the Truth and so are you. All other things can be argued, disagreed upon or changed. Who you are can never be denied and your existence can't be argued. This is for you, this is a note to yourself, from yourself, through me. This the key to realizing who you really are.

CHAPTER ONE
The Greatest Question

The greatest question you will ever have to answer in life is "who am I?"

The greatest question is not, who is Abraham, Jesus, Confucius, Buddha or Muhammad? The greatest question is not, who is God? Or, where is God? The greatest question is, "who are you?"

Although those men and concepts—when clearly understood—can help point you to who you are, they are not more important or greater than who you are.

Throughout this book, I will ask and answer this fundamental but essential question: who am I? And, I will bring to your attention that the awareness of who you are is the foundation of true success in any profession, position or purpose in life. The most important thing in life is to know yourself. All of the great leaders and teachers who've came to this planet insist that you *know thyself.*

Who am I? No really, who are you? Once this question is answered, everything else is simple and all other questions are secondary.

We live in a world that ridicules and persecutes the living but worship and praise the dead. We do this in politics, religion, sports, music, art, science and throughout history. For years, humanity has crucified their generational greats, while giving honor and respect to the dead.

Isn't it funny that while Jesus, John the Baptist, Gandhi, Abraham Lincoln, JFK, Martin Luther King Jr., Tupac, and Malcolm X were living they were ridiculed, rejected, slandered, persecuted and assassinated? They are now worshiped in their death, but they were rejected in their generation. People killed Jesus, but after his death they started a religion in his name. People killed Martin Luther King Jr. then, after his death, gave him a holiday, named schools after him and built a statue in his name.

The human ego seems to always reject the present moment—the now—and abides in the past. We even do it in rap music and sports. We worship the dead, the formers or the retired, then we criticize the people who are in their moment. How dare we compare Drake, Jay Z, Kayne, J. Cole or Kendrick Lamar to Tupac? No matter how great Lebron James, Kobe Bryant, Stephen Curry or Kevin Durant is, was or becomes, how dare we compare them to Michael Jordan? We will deny the greatness in our generation to worship and honor the past.

How dare we say Floyd Mayweather is greater than Muhammad Ali or Rocky Marciano? Even though Floyd hasn't lost a fight and is just as great, if not greater than anyone in the sport of boxing history, we wouldn't dare compare. Why is this? It is because the human ego worships the past and the dead, while rejecting and denying the greatness that is right in front of us at this very moment. But oh, how great they will be when they die—when they become the past. Then, we will honor them. Then, we will talk about how great they are.

We do the same thing at funerals, we praise them in their death but gossip about them while they are living. If you take a look at American money, what do you see? You see dead men, dead presidents. If you take a look at our religions, what do you see? You see dead men, dead prophets and spiritual teachers. Although, I do have respect for all of the leaders of the past, I am simply using this as example to illustrate a point. Here is my point:

> Anyone still alive has hope; even a living dog is better than a dead lion (Ecclesiastes 9:4).

The power is within the living; the power is the living. Our religions have done us injustice by worshiping the dead over the living. As if the living does not possess any power. Be mindful of the fact that when the truth is told, the dead only exist through the living's memory, thoughts and stories.

The word "dead" itself means not existing, gone or extinct. Dinosaurs are extinct or considered dead. Despite the fact that dinosaurs did exist, they don't exist now. No matter how strong or powerful the dinosaurs were in the past, within this paradox of the now, they have no power.

Here is what Jesus said to the religious leaders of his time:

> I can guarantee this truth: before Abraham was ever born, I am (John 8:53).

To understand this bold statement, you must

first understand the context in which he said it. Jesus was a Jew, and Abraham was considered the founder and father of the Jews (according to Judaism). As a reminder, note that Abraham was physically born before Jesus. Therefore, the religious leaders of this time were ready to stone Jesus and kill him for the statement he made. His statement was considered blasphemous and disrespectful because during the time that Jesus was on Earth, there was no one greater than Abraham and Moses, according to the Jews. Telling a Jew that you are greater than Abraham is like telling a Christian of this time you are greater than Jesus. I'm pretty sure they would be very upset and think you completely lost your mind.

Jesus said, "Before Abraham was born, I am." In other words, Jesus claimed he existed before Abraham was born. At the time, Jesus was in his early 30s.

Abraham lived and died more than a thousand years before his birth. But, this was not just a man or any man. This was Abraham, the father of the Jews. Many people thought Jesus lost his mind. But did he? Did he lose his mind or did Jesus know the answer to the question, who am I?

Even throughout Jesus' time, people considered the men of the past greater than him. It wasn't until after his death that some "claimed" he was greater. Religion is dangerous when it focuses on the past. It is very unhealthy when it does not focus on and support the power, prophets and people of the now. When Jesus was alive, they didn't have respect for him and his message like they did for the dead—Moses and Abraham. If they did, they would not have killed him.

Spirituality is only spirituality when it is a personal experience, not a story of the past that you must believe. Religion is people and stories of the past, whereas spirituality is people and experiences of the now. If religion doesn't evolve or change its focus to this generation, it will die and so will the people that remain in it. It's interesting that we say things like, "yesterday is in the tomb." Or, "forget about yesterday, you can't change the past." Yet, we seem to be immovable and focused on 2,000 years of the past. As a result, this generation is suffering tremendously. This led me to the greatest question ever…who am I?

Religion and society has led you to believe that the dead is greater, wiser, more powerful, more spiritual and more important than you are and that is simply not true. There never has, nor will it ever be anyone greater than you. Others may have more possessions, more fame, more money, more respect, more awards, more stocks, more education and more accumulations, but no one's story or life experience is less than or greater than your own. Yes, you matter! Your life and experience is valuable and the very fact that you are reading this right now is evidence that you earnestly desire to know the truth of who you are and the power you possess.

Now, focus your attention on *who you are*. Jesus, Buddha, Abraham and Muhammad are dead, no longer physical. Allegorically speaking, they were great men that realized their power. Now, it's time for you to realize yours.

If your church, religion or beliefs do not help you answer the question, *who am I*, it is meaningless and offers no value to you. I don't need to know who Moses was if it doesn't help me realize who I am. I don't need to know what God said to Peter, Paul, John or Luke. I need to know what the voice is saying to me. Only when stories from the past empower, educate and reveal to us *who we are* do they add value. Knowing that Moses parted a red sea with a stick doesn't add value to your life. Knowing that a snake told a man to eat a fruit doesn't add value to knowing who you are and why you're here. It's time for us to look to our generation for the answers. It's time to believe in the teachers, prophets, leaders, gurus, messengers and apostles of this generation—of the now. Most importantly, it is time for us to overcome our fear and quit running from the greatness that we are and the power we possess. We must ask, answer and accept this simple but life changing question: Who am I?

Who am I? Why am I here? What is my passion? What will I create? How will I help the world? These questions are more important than any diploma. They are more important than any degree.

CHAPTER TWO

Our Deepest Fear

Marianne Williamson once said, "Our deepest fear is not that we are inadequate. Our deepest fear is that we are powerful beyond measure." My search has lead me to discover why we don't focus on who we are—it is simply because of fear. We are afraid of knowing ourselves. We are afraid of the question itself.

We rely on society, parents, teachers, friends, family, social media and religion to tell us who we are. So, our belief of who we are actually comes from an external source. The sad reality is, more times than not, that outside source does not know who they are. They're only passing along unconscious information that is regurgitated generation after generation. This is why you hear things like, "I'm a child of God" or "God is my father." These statements did not come from a realization, it came from regurgitation (hearing the same information over and over again). This is the difference between enlightenment and education. Enlightenment is the realization of your own being, realizing who you are. Education is the accumulation of information you receive from someone or something else. This is why many people rather be educated than enlightened. They rather be told by someone else who they are. When you don't know who you are, you will live in fear and insecurity because we fear what we don't know. In spite of not knowing, we believe, and most of the time our beliefs are not our own. We accept the beliefs that are passed down to us. We end up believing in something, and we don't know why. When you don't know why you believe something, it's impossible for you to understand it. When you don't understand what you believe, you cannot apply it. Consequently, we have a whole generation of people who say they believe in Jesus but don't understand why. And, as a result, they can't apply his principles and teachings. This type of belief is treacherous because it came through the installation of another, instead of the realization of oneself.

We have heard many times that you can't love anyone until you love yourself. That statement is the absolute truth. But, not only can you not love another until you love yourself, you also cannot know another until you know yourself. You cannot truly know who God is until you know who you are. Do not be deceived into thinking you know someone else when you don't know yourself—the self you're with 24/7.

Fear keeps you from entering the space of knowing. Fear keeps you from asking questions. It keeps you from your true potential and power. And, it limits God to a mental thought or a belief that you were taught, instead of the realization of your own being—your own self.

In fact, the term "God" is just a concept for you to put your belief in, since you are not yet spiritually mature enough to put it in yourself. You don't yet have the courage to face yourself, that's why God is there. God is there not from your finding but from your fear. Let me be clear, if you believe that you and God are separate beings, you do not know who you are. God for you has become a Sunday school teaching, just a term to believe in because you are unaware of yourself. But once you discover and realize who you really are, the concept of God will disappear within you and, instead, emerge as you.

The reason why we say, "God is in us," is because our greatest fear is that we are powerful beyond measure. We dare not say "God *is us*," so we say "God *is in us*." By doing so, we still deny the fact that we are powerful beyond measure. We believe that some other force that is separate from us, but is simultaneously in us, is the reason why we have power. Think about that. As absurd as that is, we say these things out of ignorance. However, we don't know because we don't ask, and we don't ask because we fear knowing who we really are.

Jack Canfield said, "Everything you want is on the other side of fear." Therefore, I decided to make "I AM" part 1 of *The Book of Truth* because once you overcome the fear of knowing who you are then getting what you want will not be a problem. If you completely accept yourself, I swear that getting what you want will follow knowing who you are. This is what Jesus was telling his disciples in the gospel of Matthew:

> Seek first his kingdom and his righteousness, and all these things will be given to you as well (Matthew 6:33).

Jesus made this statement because his disciples were focused on everyday needs. The 12 disciples had quit their jobs to follow Jesus and be a part of his ministry. They were concerned about what they would eat, drink and wear. But Jesus said, "Seek the kingdom and once you understand and realized this power, everything else you want will follow." As you read this, you must understand that you cannot accept the power that you are if you fear the power that you are.

Fear isn't real, it is only real when you run from it. Once you face it, it will disappear. Just like a nightmare disappears when you awaken, fear will disappear when you face it. You must face the illusion of fear, then fear will disappear and who you really are will manifest. Marie Curie said, "Nothing in life is to be feared it is only to be understood."

The purpose of life is to create. We all create consciously or unconsciously, knowingly or unknowingly but once you realize you are the creator, your life experience will become even greater.

CHAPTER THREE

Two Sides of a Coin

There are two sides to every coin. Quarters, dimes, nickels and pennies all have two sides. In America, we call those sides heads and tails.

Take out a coin right now, just one. It can be any coin listed above. Notice there are two sides. In-spite of those two sides, it's still only one coin. It is no more or less of a coin on tails than heads and vice versa. Both heads and tails are sides of the same coin. The same is true in the universe because of duality—two sides to one reality. We call those sides many things: energy and matter, spiritual and physical, non-physical and physical, invisible and visible, unseen and seen, and the list goes on.

The word and concept "God" has been misused and misunderstood for centuries. We have made God a man. We gave God a son, and some religions made God a woman. The true God is energy, pure energy. Energy is neither male nor female within itself. Although energy can take on the form of any and all things, it is not limited to anything.

Most religions believe that God is LOVE. This doesn't mean that God is loving. Love is not a characteristic of God, love is what God is. Even better translated, I say, "Love is God." Love is neither male nor female. Love is not in or for a certain religion. Love does not choose one race over another.

The human ego created a God that is selective. A God who is angry, jealous, prejudice, racist, cruel, impatient, conditional, bipolar, selfish and exclusive. When in fact love is not selective at all, nor is it exclusive. Love includes everyone and all things. So, when I speak of God in this particular section I am speaking of pure energy. All living things are God in a different form and vibration.

Albert Einstein said, "All religions, arts and sciences are branches of the same tree." Same tree just different branches. Same energy just different vibrations. Same coin just different sides. Same God just different forms.

Now, let's take it a little deeper with the coin analogy. Bear in mind that I previously said that one coin has two sides. However, while it has two sides it is still the same coin. It is no more or less of a coin because of the side that it's on. Therefore, God is no more or less energy, seen or unseen, physical or non-physical. For that reason, regardless if it's pure energy or matter, it's immaterial or material, it is still God. Everything is God and God is everything. Everything that exists comes from the same source; everything is that source appearing and behaving differently. But, what does change are the sides, the appearance or the form.

This is why Jesus was so misunderstood because they didn't understand he was two sides to one coin. He was also Spirit—God in a body. Just like you.

Jesus said over and over in the scriptures "me

and my Father are one." One coin has two sides, but it is not two coins. In other words, he was saying, "I am the Father in physical form, I am the visible side of the Father." He also told Philip in the Book of John:

> If you have seen me, you have seen the
> father (John 14:9).

Philip wanted to know when they would see God. But Jesus replied, if you have seen me, you have seen God—the Father. You are God in physical form.

This is what the Book of Genesis refers to when it says that we are made in the image of God. "Made in the image of God" does not mean you are less than, it means you are the physical and visible manifestation of God.

If you choose to make the claim that there is only one God or the claim that you and God are one, you are not suggesting that you and God are two separate beings. You are suggesting that God and you are the heads and tails of the same coin.

Take one coin to the store and make a claim that it's two. Trust me, the cashier will not be fooled. You can flip the coin on both heads and tails and it will still only be one coin. If you have a quarter, you can't say that because it has two sides it's equal to 50 cents. Again, it's not two different quarters, it's the same coin.

God and who you really are, are one in the same. Just two different sides of the same coin. You are energy acting as matter, energy in the physical form. Your mind—your ego—will have a hard time accepting this simple truth. In fact, for some, the ego has a hard time accepting that a black man and a white man are one—equal. How dare I say God and I are one? Yes, a black man has a different appearance and maybe even a different personality than a white man. But, the simple truth is they are both human. The same is true if we take this deeper. Everything in life is life itself, only the appearance, personality and psychology is different. Yes, this is my claim: You and God are one. The ego will have you pretending to be confused and denying your own being. Be aware of your ego while reading these words. Although one coin has two sides, it can only be on one side at a time. Therefore, spirit and ego cannot exist in the same mental space. You have to choose which side you are going to live by.

Metaphorically speaking, this is why the devil isn't in heaven; God and the devil cannot exist in the same space. This is why you have heard religious people say that God kicked the devil out of heaven. The devil isn't some outside force or demon in a red suit. The devil is the negative energy and thoughts that exist within you. The devil is a symbol of fear and ego, whereas God is a symbol of love and spirit. Take notice that fear and love can't exist in the same space. For example, if you are afraid of dogs, it is impossible for you to love dogs. It is impossible for you to love something or someone you fear. Love casts out all fear, so be aware of the fear that arrives in your mind while reading this book.

Previously, I talked about how your deepest fear is that you are powerful beyond measure. The mind, your ego, fears this power. The Spirit, which you call God, knows this power. In fact, it is this power.

You may have heard people say, "It was God, it wasn't me. God did it, not me." Or, "God did it through me." But, you and God are one.

Therefore, if you did it, then God did it. If God did it, then you did too. As a matter of fact, these are just different dimensions of your own being.

It's amazing to me how when we make mistakes, we blame ourselves or the devil. When we do something good, then God is responsible. You cannot go into a courtroom and say God did it or the devil did it. You can't commit a crime and blame God or the devil. Because, the court understands that God and the devil are just dimensions within your own being or two different concepts of your own mind. What you call God and the devil are terms used to express the positive and negative energy that exist within you. What is labeled "positive" and "negative" depends on who you ask. Regardless, it is still energy that exists within you. God, the devil, heaven nor hell exist outside of you. These are all spiritual dimensions that exist within you and express themselves through you. One coin, two sides. This is the duality of reality.

I'm not speaking about the duality of yin and yang, man and woman, up and down, or good and bad. Those are dualities on Earth. I'm referencing the material and non-material world. I'm referring to the dimensions within yourself. Now, let's go into energy and matter to get a better understanding of **I AM**.

CHAPTER FOUR
Energy and Matter

Science call energy and matter what religions call spiritual and physical. Everything physical is spiritual because the spiritual is the source of the physical. Just like energy is the source of all matter. I use the example of energy and matter because they are two of the greatest concepts that I've found to describe who and what we are.

Scientists have proven that everything is energy. Everything is energy vibrating and expressing itself in different forms. All matter is energy but not all energy is matter. For example, ice is water but not all water is ice. Ice is water—liquid—in solid form. Ice is water frozen. Ice is water in a physical form or a solid state.

Just like the ice, you are God in a solid and physical form, there is truly no difference. Water in the form of liquid is a great visible example of energy. Ice is a great visible example of matter. When the ice dies or melts it becomes pure water again. When the body dies—just like the ice—you become pure energy again.

It is important to recognize that the ice is not less than or greater than the water because the ice is the water in a different form. Water is not greater than the ice because the frozen state of water is in fact ice. This can be applied to anything since science has also proved that everything in the universe is interconnected. Everything is connected. Whether it's the sun, plants, water, animals or humanity, everything is connected. By knowing this simple truth, this fact, we can now take a huge leap in spirituality.

We now know that everything from the water we drink, to the thoughts we think, to the food we eat, to the car we drive, all of it is energy. Energy cannot be created nor destroyed. Energy can only transmute and change forms. Notice that the ice never really died, it only changed from a solid form to a liquid. It transmuted from ice back to water.

The same is true for you. In life, just like the ice, you never really die. You may change forms because the body is only matter. You must understand that you are not the "form," but rather the energy underneath the form.

At funerals, you'll hear the preacher say, "They have gone to a better place." Think about it. If a body is laying in a casket, how could that person be in another place? This is true because we are not the body, we are in the form or solid state of the body. The ice was also in a solid state, it didn't die, it only went back to a liquid state.

So, when the minister says that a person is in a better place, he or she means that person is in a different state or a better form. Since, the word "better" comes from the ego, the best word to use is "different." Black is not better than white, it's simply different. White is not better than black, it's simply different. Therefore, a person just like ice does not die, they just transform to a different state. This simply means they are no longer in a solid or physical form.

It is impossible for you to die because you are energy. Energy can't die, it only changes states and appearance. Remember, it is impossible for water to die, it only changes. Can you shoot water with gun? Can you cut water with a knife? No. For that reason, water doesn't die and neither do you—the consciousness.

I use the illustration of water because everything on this planet needs water for its survival. Your body is made up of about 60 percent water, your brain of about 75 percent water, and the Earth of about 70 percent water. Consequently, water can teach us something very essential about ourselves; it's able to change forms but never dies.

Although it is a parable, Genesis Chapter 1 teaches us something about water as well. It explains that water was never created. God did not create water, it was already there in the beginning.

If water isn't a clear enough example, think of it another way. If someone cut off your foot, you wouldn't say, "I died." Why? Because you're not your foot. Therefore, if your foot was gone or cut off you wouldn't say, "I am no more. I am dead." If you wouldn't say this with your foot, why would you say this with your body?

You are not your body. Your body is just an instrument used for this physical realm. Your body is just an Earth suit, a form.

When you leave the body or lose your body, like losing the foot, why would you then say "I am dead"? Or, "They are dead"? They aren't dead, they've merely changed forms, and their body is no more. This is key to understanding who you are. You must first understand that you are not the body. The body is just a solid form of energy which allows you to operate on Earth as a human. You are pure energy. You are pure awareness.

When you realize who you really are on the deepest level, you will stop looking in the sky for God. You will look in the mirror. You will look within.

CHAPTER FIVE

You are not the Body or the Mind, You are Divine

Eckhart Tolle said, "You find peace in life not by rearranging the circumstances of your life but by realizing who you are at the deepest level."

To be ignorant of who you are, at the deepest level, is to be blind. It is to be dead. When I say blind, I am not talking about a physical blindness. When I say dead, I am not talking about a physical death. I'm speaking of unawareness and unconsciousness on the spiritual realm.

The word ignorance means blindness, unawareness or unconsciousness. Therefore, this is key to understanding Jesus' message and ministry, the kingdom of God. It is important to acknowledge that this is not a physical kingdom nor a place in the sky but rather a dimension within yourself. Heaven is not outer space or a physical place—it is a reality within you. An Egyptian proverb says, "The kingdom of heaven is within you and whosoever shall know himself shall find it." This is the same thing Jesus said in Luke 17:21. Therefore, you must recognize that this is a spiritual place or dimension.

When Jesus gave sight to the blind, it wasn't a physical blindness. In fact, the parables point to a deeper meaning. In reality Jesus was simply removing ignorance from the mind. You may have heard people say, "I once was lost, but now I'm found." Lost means to be unaware of your location. If you have heard someone say or sing this quote, I'm sure you realize that the word "lost" isn't referring to your physical location. They were not saying they were "lost" as if they needed a GPS or didn't know which city or state they were in. They say and sing this quote because they were lost in mind, lost in thought—unaware of who they really were.

The same is true with the phrase, "I am blind, but now I see." This isn't a physical blindness like Stevie Wonder or Ray Charles but rather a spiritual blindness. For most people, you've had your eye sight your entire life, since birth you could see physically.

So, when reading the teachings of Jesus be aware

that 99 percent of everything he speaks about is spiritual, not physical. He told Nicodemus in John Chapter 3 that he needs to be born again. Nicodemus said, "How can a man enter his mother's womb again when he is old." Nicodemus thought Jesus was talking about a physical birth. Jesus was talking about a spiritual and mental birth—a transformation by renewing your mind and realizing who you are.

This is also why Jesus would say over and over again "Let those who have an ear hear." Jesus knew that everyone had ears but he was saying "hear" as in understand. Just because you hear something doesn't mean you comprehend it. This is why Jesus says in Mark:

> They will see but not see and they will
> hear but not hear (Mark 4:12).

This means they will see physically but not learn. They will hear physically but not understand. Jesus parables are fables, but they are full of spiritual principles and laws.

So, what we take from these stories is that if you don't know who you really are then you are dead. You are lost, you are blind, not physically but spiritually. This is why the pop star Drake said, "Just to live doesn't mean you're alive." Those who are unaware of their true self are already dead.

The word "dead" in this context means asleep; being asleep is a state of death. When Jesus raised the dead and healed the blind, it was not a physical transformation. He gave sight to those who were blind to who they really were. This goes back to our initial question. Now, really pause for a second and ask yourself, "Who am I?" I'm not asking your name or your purpose. Your answer shouldn't be something you were told or something you heard from some religion. Who are you really? Who is the one behind the body, behind the eyes, behind the mind?

One day, I came to the realization that I am not the body. I was in a room alone in complete silence. I looked around the room and began to look at everything in it. I looked at my phone, my books, my clothes, my shoes and my bed. While observing these objects, I realized something very simple. I realized that none of these objects could move. The only thing in the room that was moving was me. The books didn't move, my phone nor my bed could move. None of these things could move unless I moved them myself.

Then, it hit me. I am not my body. And, when

I leave this body, it won't move. When you leave the body, your body will no longer move. It's just like these objects, it can't move unless you move it. You are the one behind the body.

Have you been to a funeral? I'm sure you have. The person that is dead or no longer in the body, cannot move the body. This is why they have morticians move it because that person is no long present.

The proof you are not the body is that one day you will leave it. But, how can you leave something that you are? You can only leave something that you are not and you are not the body. You can leave your phone, your keys, your house and again, even your body but you can never leave yourself.

I know this the funeral life pretty well. Growing up, my family owned their own funeral home. I worked there on and off for about 10 years. It made me aware of a few things. It made me realize everything that has a beginning also has an end. It made me realize that the body is simply an "Earth vehicle" that came from the Earth and must go back to the Earth. Your body has a beginning and an end.

Because you are energy, there is no end to you. There was no beginning to you. The end of your body is not the end of you. You are the one behind the body, you are not the body. The same is true for your mind. You are not the mind. Your body is an instrument of the mind. Your mind is an instrument of awareness —that which you are. The mind controls the body and you control the mind. At least that is the way it was meant to be designed. However, more times than not, people allow the mind to control them.

An instrument that is designed to be used by you is now using you and even pretending to be you. In order for this problem to be fixed humanity must become aware and drop this mind-body identification. Then, and only then, is peace, awareness, oneness and heaven on Earth possible.

The mind when used properly is a beautiful tool of creation. The body when used properly is a beautiful vehicle for action and manifestation. The issue comes only with the false identification. Most people realize they are not the body because it's easy to see and understand. But, most of humanity believes they are the mind, they believe they are their thoughts.

If you ever try meditating, you realize you are not your thoughts. Your thoughts won't shut up. You will be thinking about what you're going to do after meditation. Your mind will think of a person or a task you need to do. It will even think about not thinking, just to continue thinking. It will think about the past or the future just to escape the present moment because this moment is where God is. This eternal moment of the now is where salvation is.

You cannot reach salvation and God in the past or the future because the past and future are concepts of the mind. God is divine and you cannot reach God through the mind. Mind requires time and God is timeless. The mind only knows what it has heard, read, experienced or learned. This is why a newborn baby doesn't believe anything at all—it has not yet been taught or heard the stories of God.

A child doesn't come to Earth with beliefs and

more times than not their beliefs are forced upon them. No child is born Christian or Muslim, racist or prejudice; these are things that they're taught. Children don't believe in a particular religion, they are taught by family, society or their environment. You weren't born believing the English language; you were taught it. You weren't born thinking one plus one equals two; you were taught it. So, understand this fundamental truth: The mind cannot know God because God is behind and beyond the mind. The mind can only know what's in front of it.

Take your face for example, you cannot see your face. You can see the face of others, but you cannot see your face. Unless you're in front of a mirror, then you will only see a reflection of your face. The reason you can't see your face is because you are behind your face. You are seeing through your eyes, behind the face.

If you ever put on a mask for Halloween, or any other event, this would be clear to you. You are the one behind the mask; you are not the mask. This is an example of God and the mind. God is behind the mind. The mind cannot know or see God, it cannot know your true self—the source. God—who you really are—can see the mind and the thoughts that goes on inside you, but the mind can never see what's behind it. It can see the body, it can see everything that appears to be outside of you, including trees, people, animals, cars and food. But, it cannot see God. This is why the bible says, "No man has seen God" because man *is* the mind. No mind has ever seen God because this is absolutely impossible.

The mind believes in God because it does not know God. It is impossible for it to know God, so instead it creates beliefs and fictions about God. The mind fears what it doesn't know and understand. But, God isn't something for you to believe in; God is something for you to realize within yourself. You can know God but it is impossible to believe in God, because belief deals with mind and the mind is incapable of this. If you have to "believe" in your God, then your God is a fiction, a fable. God is simply a story, simply words from a book and you have to "believe" words. Words are *God of the mind,* and God itself is just a word. If you "know" God you don't need a story about it. You don't need words about something you already know. You need stories for things you do not know. The mind is behind the body and you—God—are behind the mind.

Listen, I'm not trying to get you to believe that you are awareness because at this level beliefs won't help.

Beliefs come from words, and you don't need to believe something you know. You don't need a book or scriptures for something you know, and you don't need a book on a person you have experienced for yourself.

Take a friend for instance, or a parent, or anyone you have spent a lot of time with, you don't need a book about them; you know them through experience. Even if you read a book about this person, it would be based on someone else's experience with them. For this reason, I don't need a book about my dad. If my sister wrote about him, I know it would be according to her experience. I have my own experiences with him, therefore words and stories are unnecessary. Stories are for beliefs and the mind, not the spirit and experience. The same is true for the scriptures. They are according to Jeremiah, Luke, Matthews and John. You cannot know God through the stories or words of another person, dead or alive. You cannot know Jesus through Luke, and you cannot know Jesus through Matthew; that is their own experience.

Let me make it a little clearer for you. Say you are in a relationship with someone, and you tell your friend great things and stories about the person you're in relationship with. You tell them he or she is so amazing, patient, loving and caring. After telling these stories, your friend begins to cry and say, "Oh, how I love them. I love them so much. I don't know what I'll do without them." Now, you would look at your friend like they were crazy because they never talked to this person. They never had an experience with this person. They never seen them face to face, but they say they love them. You would think they would need to go to a mental institution. But it's truly no different than those who read stories of Luke, Moses and Matthew, and then say "I love God." How? Through the stories and words of people you never met? Think about it. People claiming to know and love God through stories and words of a person they have never met.

This is dangerous because it is impossible for the mind to know God. You can only come to God when the mind is dropped. That's why meditation is a technique of self-realization, realizing yourself as awareness. When thinking stops, then you meet God. God is beyond both books and beliefs. God is beyond both thoughts and words.

Even the words on these pages are not the truth because the truth cannot be put into words.

What religions, scriptures, teachers and masters do with words is attempt to point people to the truth. The bible is not the truth, it is symbolic stories and parables designed to help point you to the truth. But the words within themselves will never be the truth because to reach the truth you have to go beyond words.

Words are for the mind. Words are like seeds and your mind is like the ground. So, there's no way you can get to this place through stories, words and thoughts. All words emerge from the mind and are created for the mind. Therefore, you have to realize you are not the mind, and you are not the body. You are the awareness that is beyond and behind. You are the divine.

While searching for God I found myself. While searching for myself I found the truth. Then I realized I AM Truth. I realized I AM God.

CHAPTER SIX

You are God Pretending to be a Human Being

Many different words are used to point to that which we are. Words like consciousness, awareness, energy, source, higher self, and many others attempt to describe the divine—that which can't be defined. But the word "God" creates so much tension in people. It creates so much confusion, frustration and fear.

People have been taught different myths and stories about what God is and what God isn't. That's why when the term is used it creates a lot of confusion. Someone else's definition may contradict what you were taught or told.

So, when I say that you are God pretending to be a human being, I'm saying exactly what the philosopher Pierre Teilhard De Chardin said: "We are not human beings having a spiritual experience. We are spiritual beings having a human experience." God is Spirit, and we are God having a human experience—energy expressing itself in human form.

When I say you are God pretending to be a human being. I mean you are energy, consciousness. You are the source, truth and awareness. I am not saying you're the Christian

God, the Muslim God, the Jewish God or any Biblical God because these gods were created by the human ego. Man created these Gods attempting to define something that can't be defined. So no, I am not speaking of the God they talk about in a church or in a temple. I'm speaking of something beyond that. I'm saying you are the source. You are the watcher. You are the awareness, and you are the energy that is underneath both the mind and the body. You are the awareness that watches over your thoughts. You are the awareness that never changes. Your body will change, your mind will change, but you are the one that was there when your body was 3 years old. You are the one that was there when your body was 10 years old. You are the one that is present reading this right now.

Over time, your physical parts will age and

change. You don't think like you thought in middle school, but you are the same watcher of your life. You are the being that exists in all forms and the one that appears as all forms—that is who you really are. These words are not meant to be believed, rather point you to the one being that you already are.

Remember the mind needs words, but the Spirit knows all things. You may have heard "God knows all things," the Spirit that you are knows all things. This part of you is connected to your intuition, and this part of you has the answer to every question and a solution for every problem. This part of you does not need any words or thoughts. The mind needs to be educated and taught, but this part of you *knows all things* because it is all things. Therefore, everything is the same thing appearing and pretending to be something different. Take a look at these questions:

- What is God?

- What is Life?

- What is Love?

- What are You?

Aren't these answers one in the same? The last three questions answer the first, and the first question answers the last three. What is Life? God. What is Love? God. What are You? God. What is God? Life, Love and You.

- Life – is God experienced

- Love – is God expressed

- You – are God in the flesh

God is everything: life, love and you. You are God pretending to be a human being. You are the source and reflection of all things.

Let's go a little deeper, and I'll help you understand why I say you are God pretending to be a human being.

Take cartoons for instance. They are not really cartoons. What I mean by that is cartoons are humans pretending to be cartoons. Notice that I said you are God pretending to be a human being. A cartoon is a human pretending to be a cartoon. There's a person or actor behind every cartoon. These animated creations came directly from the human imagination. They are only the imagination and creation of humans.

If you watch the movie *The Lion King*, you know the lion figures are just creations of human beings. This is why they act, talk and think as if they are human. If you've ever seen *Planet of the Apes*, *A Bug's Life*, *Cars* or any television cartoons that act and talk as if they're human, it is because humans are acting as those cartoons.

They say man is made in the image of God. In actuality, God is made in the image of man. The God of the religions is a God with human attributes. This term in theology is called "anthropomorphous," it is to put human attributes and characteristics on a deity, being or thing that is not human. This why we say God is a man. We say he's a father and He has a son. We even say God is jealous, and we say the hand of God is on me. But God is Spirit and Spirit doesn't have a hand. Spirit is not a man.

All of the writers of the bible are male, this is why they made God a male. They made God in their image. Even the Book of Ruth was not written by Ruth, it was written by a male. So, the God you were taught about came from the imagination of man.

If we look at the word "create," it means to evolve from one's own thoughts or imagination. Therefore, to say that God created you is to say that you are made up, that you are not real nor different than the cartoon—that you came from the imagination of God.

One day I was having a conversation with a girl and I asked her, "Are cartoons real?" Her response was "No." I immediately asked her, "Why not? They exist, they have their own TV shows, movies and reality, so how are they not real?" She replied, "They are not real because they were made up." I paused and said to her, "So you mean to tell me cartoons aren't 'real' because someone made them up? Because someone created them?" "Yes," she said. "Well, what about God?" I asked. "The bible says God created you, so in other words you are made up too? Are you not real?" Immediately, her energy changed and her ego and emotions went wild. She said, "Yes, I am real. I know I am real. God made me, but I am real." So, I responded, "Then why aren't the cartoons real? They were created and made up. From this point of view, you are no different than them." She followed with, "But that's different, you can't compare that to God."

She couldn't accept this. But, if she would have accepted this simple truth, she would have freed herself that day. I didn't compare God to cartoons, I simply used the word "create" in relation to cartoons. Therefore, if you claim God created you, you are also saying you're made up.

If in the beginning there was only one God, then the only thing that is real is God. God is the only thing that really exists. Everything came from the imagination of God, and that's why the Bible calls everything the creation of God. But the question you would have to stop and ask yourself is this: "Who is real, Me or God?" One is made up, one is created, one is not real and one is pretending just like the cartoon. There cannot be two different realities. Reality is one. God is one. So, the question now becomes, who is created? Who is made up? Who is present reading this right now God or me? Who is the one making all of my choices in life God or me? Whose imagination does this come from God's or mine?

You can look at this from two different perspectives: you can say we are human pretending to be God, or you can say we are God pretending to be human. You have to accept one because there cannot be two realities or two different existences, that is impossible.

Open your eyes, humans have been pretending to be many things. Humans have been pretending to be The Tooth Fairy, Santa Claus, The Boogeyman, Batman, Spiderman, The Easter Bunny, and the list goes on. People have been pretending to be all these things. It should not bother you when I say you are God pretending to be a human being. Humans pretend to be Santa. Humans pretend to be the Tooth Fairy. If you can fully understand and accept this lesson, you will have a clear picture of who you really are.

In the beginning, the only thing that existed was God. Everything else was created, it was made up and came from God's imagination. In actuality, there is nothing else but God. Anything else is just a form appearing in God's imagination. Whereas God is all things pretending and appearing to be everything.

And you are God impersonating a human being.

CHAPTER SEVEN

"I AM" the Only Thing That Exists

I am the only thing that exists. Yes, "I AM" is the only thing that exists.

What is I AM?

I AM is pure consciousness, pure energy and pure awareness. Therefore, consciousness is the only thing that exists. Awareness is the only thing that exists. Energy is the only thing that exists. They are just different words and labels pointing to the same reality.

If someone says, "I am energy," you would be okay with that. If someone says, "I am God," your ego would immediately go on the defense (unless you already know that you are God). But, if you aren't aware of that which you are, you would be upset upon hearing this statement. The reason being is this would contradict what your religion, parents, society and government say of God.

In the mind, I AM is considered a crime. This is why Jesus died. They murdered Jesus because he came into this awareness that I AM. This is scientifically proven that everything is the same thing vibrating and appearing different. Don't be deceived by the appearance, the beliefs, the behavior, the social status or any mind-body identification. I AM is the only thing that exists.

Many people would accept it if I said "God is

the only thing that exists." But in Exodus, God tells Moses:

> I am sending you to Pharaoh so that you can bring my people Israel out of Egypt (3:10-15).

Then, Moses said to God, "Who am I that I should go to Pharaoh and bring the people of Israel out of Egypt?" God answers, "I will be with you. And this will be the proof that I sent you. When you bring the people out of Egypt, all of you will worship God on this mountain." Moses replies to God, "Suppose I go to the people of Israel and say to them, the God of your ancestors has sent me to you, and they ask me, what is his name? What should I tell them?" God answered Moses, "I AM WHO I AM. This is what you must say to the people of Israel, I AM has sent me to you."

Okay, let's make a few things clear, we have principles hidden in fables. Everything has awareness in it, including cartoons, books, movies, plants, animals and everything in existence. You have to discern what is from ego, the mind, and what is from awareness, the source. We know God doesn't have a chosen "people." God doesn't like Israel more than Egypt, Egypt more than China, and so forth. Love is inclusive. Love is for all. And although this story is a parable, it has a principle behind the parable. A parable is an allegory, a myth, a tale, a fiction that is used to illustrate a point and a principle.

If you are confused about this chapter, please read the introduction of this book over and over until you understand how I use terms like God, Jesus and the Bible interchangeably to point to a principle.

God told Moses "I AM." Who is God? I AM. Read this with awareness and you will answer both the question of who you are and who God is. Who is God? I AM. I AM God.

Look at the question, "Who am I?" Now, read the question backwards and you will have your answer. I AM who? I AM who God is. God is who? I AM.

It is impossible for I AM not to be. The word "am" itself means to be or to exist. So, if you exist now, you always have and you always will in some shape, state or form.

Everything in existence came from one source, no matter what name you choose give it. Everything in existence is that one source. Everything in existence is existence itself.

Think about this example, if you get a Christian in

a room with a Jew, Muslim, New-ager, Buddhist and Atheist, they would argue over the existence of God. One thing they couldn't argue over is the existence of you. It is evident and clear that you exist. Why would God be the argument instead of you? It's because in this context the term "God" is being used as a mental idol, a mental illusion. "God" requires belief, but you don't require a belief because there is evidence that you exist. The very fact that you are present dissolves all arguments.

Imagine if someone rings your doorbell, and you go to the door to say "I am not here." The very fact that you've spoken is proof that you are there. You can't deny yourself. While you may deny a God, you still cannot deny the fact that you exist. It is time for you to realize who you are. Wake up, you are God. You are beyond the body. You are beyond the mind. You are beyond thought, and you are pure energy, pure awareness. This is why the church says your body is a temple of God. You are not the temple. Your body is the temple. You are God in the temple, in the body.

The reason we say "God is in us" is out of fear because we fail to realize what we're truly saying. Think deeply about this, when a woman is pregnant with a child, the child is in her. So, who is greater? Her or the child? Or, the better question is, how could the child exist without the mother that it's in? The child exists through the mother, without the mother the child couldn't exist. For that reason, those who claim "God is in you" are truly saying that, just like the child, God exists through you. So, without you there could be no God? Think about it. How could the child exist without the mother that it's in?

Jesus says, "The kingdom of God is in you, God is in you, therefore without you God couldn't exist." So, here is the evolution. Moses said, "God is with you." Jesus said, "God is in you." I say, "God is you."

You are two sides to one coin. You are God pretending to be a human being. You are Spirit manifested in physical form. You are the consciousness that *is* and appears as everything. You are the source, the watcher, the awareness, the existence. Realizing this is vital to true peace and happiness. Happiness and peace is a byproduct of knowing who you really are. The goal of life is to enjoy every moment. The purpose of life is to create. The mission of life is to realize who you really are. The mission of life is to realize you are life itself. Beyond your body, beyond your name, degrees, profession, career, personality, zodiac sign, and even your own mind, you are divine. I'll ask one last time. Who are you?

87

Life is a game
because God is
everything.

www.ingramcontent.com/pod-product-compliance
Lightning Source LLC
Chambersburg PA
CBHW071744090426
42738CB00011B/2557